PUFFIN BOOKS

NATURE FILE

Do you know what humans have in common with fish? Did you know that a shark has to keep swimming even when it's asleep? Have you ever heard of a tuatara?

The animal kingdom is a fascinating world and here's a book that will help you learn about fish, amphibians, reptiles, birds and mammals. Each chapter looks at the way the different groups of animals feed and behave; how their bodies work and at some of their extraordinary names! There's a list of factfile words at the end of each chapter, together with an illustrated puzzle which will test your knowledge.

A lively, informative and stimulating wildlife adventure.

Peter Hayward lives in Stirling and is Head of Biology in a Scottish Secondary School. He has written programmes for schools' television, but this is his first book to be published.

Scoular Anderson lives in Glasgow and is the author and illustrator of *A Plunder of Pirates*, *The Puffin Book of Royal London* and *Land Ahoy!*, all published in Puffin.

Nature File
Fascinating Animal Facts

Peter Hayward

Illustrated by
Scoular Anderson

PUFFIN BOOKS

For Hilary and Sam

PUFFIN BOOKS
Published by the Penguin Group
Penguin Books Ltd, 27 Wrights Lane, London W8 5TZ, England
Penguin Books USA Inc., 375 Hudson Street, New York, New York 10014, USA
Penguin Books Australia Ltd, Ringwood, Victoria, Australia
Penguin Books Canada Ltd, 10 Alcorn Avenue, Toronto, Ontario, Canada M4V 3B2
Penguin Books (NZ) Ltd, 182–190 Wairau Road, Auckland 10, New Zealand

Penguin Books Ltd, Registered Offices: Harmondsworth, Middlesex, England

First published 1992
10 9 8 7 6 5 4 3 2 1

Text copyright © Peter Hayward, 1992
Illustrations copyright © Scoular Anderson, 1992
All rights reserved

The moral right of the author and illustrator has been asserted

Printed in England by Clays Ltd, St Ives plc
Filmset in Palatino

Except in the United States of America, this book is sold subject to the condition that it shall not, by way of trade or otherwise, be lent, re-sold, hired out, or otherwise circulated without the publisher's prior consent in any form of binding or cover other than that in which it is published and without a similar condition including this condition being imposed on the subsequent purchaser

Contents

Chapter 1
Fins and Scales
Fish 7

Chapter 2
Croakers and Hoppers
Amphibians 27

Chapter 3
Snappers and Coilers
Reptiles 39

Chapter 4
Feathers and Flight
Birds 59

Chapter 5
Horns and Hair
Mammals 76

Chapter 1
Fins and Scales
Fish

What is a fish?
A fish is an animal with a backbone, scales on its skin and which breathes using gills.

FISH HISTORY

Fish have been around for a very long time. The first fish swam in the sea over 500 million years ago, give or take the odd day. They were the first animals in the world to have backbones. All other animals with backbones, including humans, are descended from fish.

The earliest fish were small. They lived on the bottom of the sea and sucked up dead plants and animals. They had to suck up their food because they didn't have jaws to bite with. These early fish were called 'jawless fish', and two kinds are still alive today. No, they aren't 500 million years old, but they do look like fish that were alive millions of years ago. The lamprey looks a bit like a snake. It has a mouth like a sucker and inside the sucker are lots of small teeth. The lamprey sticks itself on to the side of another fish and eats it alive.

Hoovering up your food is all right, but biting is even better, so fish changed and most of them grew jaws. The first things they ate were nearly all the fish without jaws. One more change brings us up to date. Some fish changed their

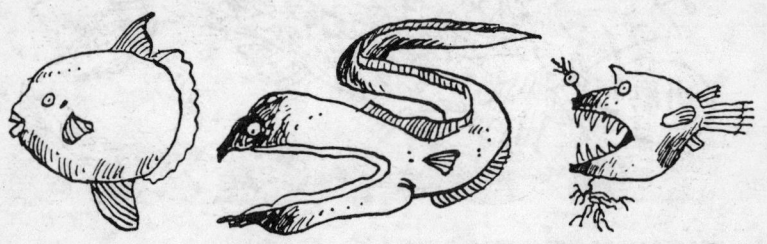

bones for cartilage. (Cartilage is the rubbery gristle in your ears and nose.) The rest of the fish kept their bones. So that leaves us with the three kinds of fish alive today. Jawless fish, fish with cartilage, like the sharks and rays, and all the rest, which are bony fish.

FISH BODIES

Because fish have been around for so long they have tried all kinds of shapes and sizes of body.

Some fish are enormous. The biggest of all is the whale-shark. It can be 18m. long and weigh as much as three and a half elephants. Don't panic – it's not a super 'Jaws'; it feeds on tiny sea creatures that it strains from seawater. In fact, it doesn't have any teeth at all.

Some fish are tiny. The smallest is the dwarf pygmy goby, which is about 9mm. long. This fish is so small that 7,000 of them weigh as much as a bag of crisps.

Whatever shape or size they are, fish have many things in common. They have scales on their bodies. Bony fish have scales that fit to-

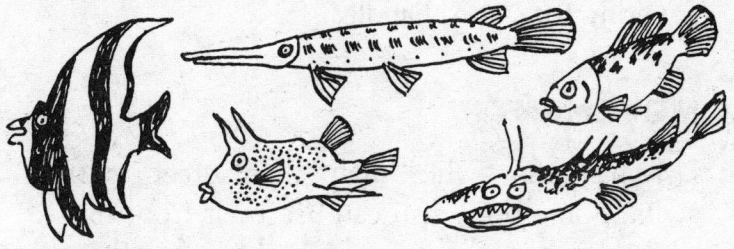

gether like the tiles on a roof. As a fish grows the number of scales it has stays the same. To stop any gaps appearing, each scale has to grow. If you look at a scale under a microscope you can see growth rings, like the rings of a tree. As with trees you can tell the age of a fish by counting the rings.

Sharks and rays have special scales like teeth all over their bodies. They are made of the same material as our teeth. Shark skin is as rough as sandpaper and in the past was used as a non-slip covering for sword handles.

MOVEMENT

Fish have fins which help them steer as they swim. Some bony fish can use their front fins to go backwards. Sharks and rays have fins that are different. Their fins are more like wings. They steer the fish as it moves forwards, but they can't be used to go backwards. What's more, a shark can't even stop. If a shark stops, it sinks, but if a bony fish stops swimming it stays still. Bony fish have special bags inside their bodies called swim-bladders, which they can blow up or let down. If a fish blows up its bag the fish goes up, if it lets gas out the fish goes down; or it can adjust the bag so it just hangs in the water. Sharks don't have swim-bladders, so they sink.

But that's not all. If a bony fish stops swimming it can still breathe using its gills. But if a shark stops swimming it drowns. Sharks swim with their mouths open and push water over their gills as they go forwards. If they stop, their gills don't work and they drown, so sharks have to keep moving. They even swim when they are asleep.

Why don't bony fish drown when they stop? Because they blow water over their gills using their mouths, even if they stop or go backwards. What's so special about going backwards? Well, for fish that nibble away at rocks for their food, or hide in small spaces, going backwards is a useful skill!

Flying out of the water altogether might seem even more difficult than going backwards, but some fish can do it. Flying hatchet fish of South America beat their front fins so fast that they fly out of the water. Flying fish that live in the sea can't really fly but they are expert gliders. If they are being chased by other fish they swim very fast and take off at 64 k.p.h. They can glide for about 1,000m. before they land. This escape plan works with most enemies; unfortunately, dolphin fish follow the flying fish and catch them when they land.

But fish don't *have* to fly to escape being eaten.

The porcupine puffer fish looks like a normal fish, but when it is in danger it blows itself up like a football. Spiny scales on its body stick out, and most other fish leave it alone. The Japanese are fond of eating a certain kind of puffer fish called the death puffer. There is one small problem — unless the fish is very carefully prepared it

can be poisonous. Every year about 20 people die from eating this fish. The Japanese call puffer meat *fugu*.

DEFENCE

Many fish use poison to defend themselves, including the most poisonous fish of all, a stone-fish called horrida. It is a very ugly fish that hides in stones on the sea bed. If you step on this fish it raises spines on its back that are sharp enough to go through beach shoes. The spines inject a poison that is so powerful it can kill people.

Scorpion-fish, unlike the stone-fish, are very beautiful. They have long, brightly coloured fins and a row of long spines on their backs. The scorpion-fish swims slowly and is not worried about enemies. The reason it is not afraid is because no fish dares eat it. The spines on its back can inject a very powerful poison. Even when it is dead the spines can still work, so they have to be cut off before the fish can be sold as food.

Sting-rays are flat fish with long tails. The tails are not used for swimming; instead rays use their tails to defend themselves. Somewhere on the tail is a sting, sometimes more than one. The sting is like a bony needle. If a sting-ray is attacked, it lashes its tail from side to side and

tries to cut and stab the enemy with its sting. As if that isn't enough, the sting has grooves in it filled with a poison which is strong enough to kill a person. Some swimmers have been killed by sting-rays they have stepped on by accident.

FEEDING

The Atlantic torpedo ray has an even more unusual weapon. It swoops down on small shellfish and then kills them with an electric shock. It's not surprising that the other name for this fish is the electric ray. Once it has given out a shock the ray takes some time to recharge its batteries before it can do it again.

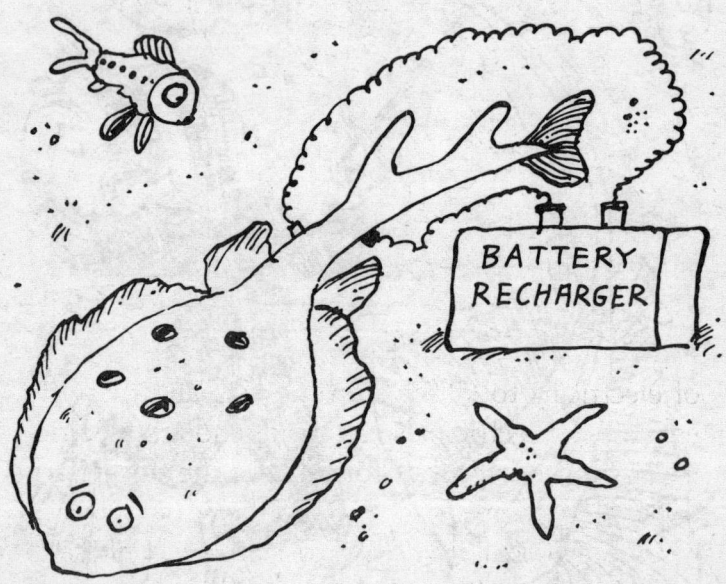

Torpedo rays aren't the most electric of fish. That record belongs to the electric eel. Electric eels make electricity using special muscles in their bodies. These eels, which can grow up to 2m. long, live in muddy water in rivers. Because the water is so murky the eels can't use their small eyes to see where they are going; instead they send out small electric currents. Using the current, the eels 'feel' their way about. If another fish swims by the eel can release a huge amount

of electricity to kill or stun the fish, and then the eel eats it. Electric eels can make enough electricity to stun horses, but fortunately they don't try to swallow them!

One fish that *would* try to swallow a horse is the tiger-shark. It's called 'the dustbin of the sea', because it tries to eat almost anything it comes across. Tiger-sharks have been known to eat car number-plates, petrol cans and wooden boxes as well as other sharks!

Sharks hunt by smell. They can follow very small amounts of blood in water till they find an injured fish. When they attack they close their eyes, so you can't poke a shark in the eye and swim away. But, if the shark has its eyes shut, how does it know when to bite? Easy — it senses the small amounts of electric current around its prey and works out when to bite from that. It's the same kind of 'feeling' that electric eels use.

A shark's bite is very much worse than its bark. A shark may have hundreds of razor-sharp teeth in its mouth. Some of the teeth are spares, waiting to replace teeth that are broken or that fall out. As the teeth are lost, new teeth move forwards so the shark always has a perfect set.

The shark with the most impressive set of teeth is the great white shark. It is the largest shark. One caught off Cuba was 6.4m. long and weighed more than two cart-horses. The great white shark is also the largest meat-eating fish in the sea. Sometimes it even eats people and it has been known to attack small boats.

The piranha is another fish famous for its bite. Piranhas live in rivers in South America. They have special teeth for biting. The teeth have sharp points to go through tough skin and razor-sharp edges which can cut through meat and even bone. One piranha on its own can't eat very much, but piranhas travel in enormous shoals or packs. A pack of piranhas can eat an enormous amount of food very quickly.

Not all fish have fearsome teeth. The archer-fish manages quite well without any at all. Archer-fish feed on insects floating on water. If they spot an insect on a leaf above the water they can shoot a jet of water from their mouths and knock the insect into the water. Once in the water it's snapped up. Archer-fish can hit insects 1.5m. above the water. If the insect is close enough, the archer-fish can leap up to 30cm. into the air to snatch it from plant leaves.

The arawana is another fish that leaps at the chance of food. It jumps out of the water and can catch bats or small birds flying just above the surface of the water.

Some fish can stay out of water for quite a while. Mud skippers crawl about on muddy beaches using their front fins as legs. Lung-fish in Africa live in an area where ponds and lakes dry up when the rain stops. If they are caught in a pond that's about to disappear they can drag themselves hundreds of metres over land to find another pond in which to swim. They don't come to any harm out of water because they have lungs as well as gills. If a lung-fish is trapped in a small pond it burrows into the mud at the bottom of the pond. It makes a small hole and covers itself with slime to stay damp. Lung-fish can stay like this for months until the rains come again and the pond fills with water.

If a fish that walks on land is odd, what about the climbing perch. This is a fish that has been found climbing trees in search of food!

Young discus fish don't have to look very far for food. They just swim up to their mother or father and nibble off a piece of skin. It isn't as bad as it sounds. The parents make a special kind of slime in their skins. The young fish eat the slime for about four weeks till they are old enough to find food for themselves.

The banded yellow cichlid fish is another fish that takes great care of its young. But this time it's the young fish that are eaten instead of their parents. If an enemy comes near, the mother sucks the baby fish into her mouth. They stay inside her mouth until the danger has passed. The full name for this fish is the banded yellow mouth-breeder. It is called this because it breeds, or looks after, its eggs inside the mother fish's mouth.

The mother fish lays her eggs on the sandy bottom of a lake. She then sucks the eggs into her mouth to keep them safe. When they hatch the young are blown out of the mother's mouth. They don't go far at first and go back inside at night or when it's dangerous to be outside.

It's not always the mother that looks after the young; sometimes it's the father. Father sticklebacks build a nest for the mother to lay her eggs in. He looks after the eggs by keeping away enemies that might try to eat them, and he fans the eggs with fresh water to keep them alive.

A sea-horse father does even more. He has a pouch on his front like the pouch of a kangaroo. The mother puts her eggs into the pouch, where they begin to grow. The father makes a special liquid in the pouch which is food for the young sea-horses. When they have grown enough, the father squeezes the young out of the pouch and they swim away.

Factfile **Fish Words**

Cartilage
A rubbery gristle. The joints in our arms and legs have cartilage in them, as well as our ears and noses.

Fugu
The meat of the puffer fish. It is eaten in Japan and has to be prepared by specially trained cooks.

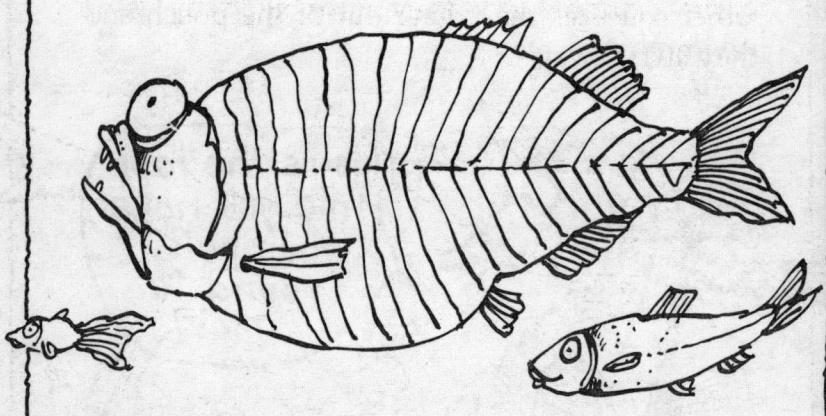

Gills
The part of a fish's body used for breathing. Gills in fish are hidden under flaps or behind gill-slits.

Jawless fish
A group of fish which don't have jaws even though they do have teeth.

Scales
The flat plates that grow from the skin of fish. Scales are also found on reptiles and on some insects.

Shoal
The name for a large number of fish swimming together.

Swim-bladder
A bag inside the body of bony fish that helps it go up or down. Sharks do not have a swim-bladder, so they sink if they stop swimming.

Can you remember some of the strange fish names in this chapter?

The pictures below will give you a clue.

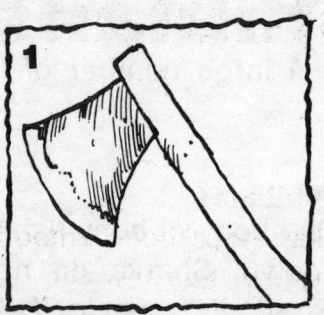

Answers on page 92

Chapter 2

Croakers and Hoppers
Amphibians

What is an amphibian?
An amphibian has a backbone, smooth skin and nearly always lays its eggs in water.

TYPES OF AMPHIBIAN

Amphibians are closely related to fish. The word amphibian means being able to live on land as well as in water. Most amphibians live on land but have to return to the water to lay their eggs.

There are three kinds of amphibians: newts and salamanders, which have tails; frogs and toads, which don't have tails; and caecilians, which are like fat worms. Caecilians are blind and mostly live in soil. Some can grow to 1.3m. long, but most are short. They are the only amphibians to have scales buried in their smooth skins.

AMPHIBIAN BODIES

The smooth skin of amphibians isn't waterproof like the skin of reptiles (see Chapter 3). Water can go through their skins. A frog in a wet place lets in water, but if a frog moves to a dry place it will dry out, which is why frogs live in damp places. Toads have a warty skin but are really frogs underneath. Every few weeks in summer a toad grows a new skin. It scrapes off the old one and eats it!

The skin of amphibians also helps them breathe. In winter, frogs can stay under water for months on end, just using their skins to breathe.

In fact, amphibians have three ways of breathing. When they are young they have gills like a fish and they breathe through their gills under water. When they become adults amphibians have lungs like us. When they are active they breathe using their lungs. If they are resting then they can use their skins.

HUNTING

By sitting very still and not moving, not even breathing, frogs can surprise their victims. Frogs hunt insects using their good eyesight. They only see moving insects, so insects that sit still escape. If an insect is seen, the frog flicks out its long sticky tongue and pulls the insect back into its mouth.

When frogs swallow they blink their eyes. This is because they are using their eyeballs to squash the insect inside their mouths. Imagine being able to feel the backs of your eyes with your tongue. Ugh!

Newts and salamanders find their food by smell and they catch it in their jaws with a swift bite. The bite has to be quick because newts and salamanders can't run very fast. Frogs can't run either, but they can jump. Frogs jump so well because their back legs are very long. In frog-jumping competitions frogs have jumped over 10m. using three jumps. Toads hardly ever jump.

Frogs can swim well in water, getting most of the push from their back legs. Newts swim using their tails; if they are moving slowly they simply walk across the bottom of the pond.

DEFENCE

As well as looking for food, amphibians have to make sure they aren't going to be lunch for someone else. Amphibians are food for many other creatures and so have found lots of ways of defending themselves.

If you can't be seen you can't be eaten. Many amphibians are coloured and patterned to look like parts of plants or stones. But some are the very opposite. They are brightly coloured and stand out from their background. These amphibians don't mind being seen because they are all poisonous. Brightly coloured frogs and salamanders use their colours to advertise the fact that they are poisonous. An animal that tries to eat a coloured frog for the first time remembers the burning taste and leaves the next one well alone.

The best known of the coloured frogs are the arrow frogs. They have very poisonous skins. Natives in South America collect the poison from the skins of frogs and use it to coat their arrows or blow-darts. All arrow frogs are small, but the golden poison arrow frog still contains enough poison to kill 20,000 mice.

Newts may be poisonous too. The spiny newt has a strange way of using its poison. When it is squeezed, its ribs burst bags of poison in its skin and the animal that's eating it gets a nasty shock. Other shock tactics are used by frogs and toads. If a toad is being attacked by a grass snake it puffs itself up and stands on tiptoe. The snake thinks the toad is too big to eat and leaves it alone.

Some frogs use colour to shock. On top the frogs are a dull colour, but when an enemy comes near they roll over to show their brightly coloured tummies. Animals know that bright colours mean poison and leave them alone.

Amphibian adults can use colours and poison to defend themselves but tadpoles and eggs also need to be kept safe from creatures that want to eat them.

EGGS

Frog-spawn is a clump of jelly-covered eggs. The record number of eggs is laid by Woodhouse's toad, which lays over 25,000 eggs at a time. If an enemy finds them, it won't be able to eat them all, so in this case it's large numbers that are the defence. Newts don't lay as many eggs as that but they do take more care of them. Each egg is stuck on the leaf of a water-plant. As the mother lays it she bends the leaf over and hides the egg. As a rule, the more care amphibians take with their eggs the smaller the number they need to lay.

The Brazilian blacksmith frog builds small private ponds made of mud to lay its eggs in. The eggs and tadpoles are kept safe from fish. Eventually the ponds are washed away by the rain and the tadpoles swim into the river.

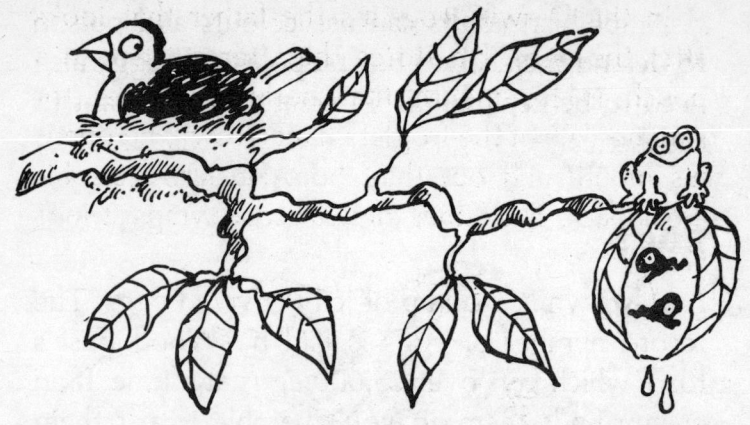

Some frogs make it even harder for enemies by laying their eggs in trees! The frogs choose a leaf which is hanging over water. The mother lays her eggs in a slimy liquid which the parents beat into a foam using their legs. The eggs hatch and the tadpoles live in the foam for a while. Eventually they fall into the water or are washed off by the rain. Once in the river they are in danger, but at least they were safe when they were very small.

Some frogs give their young an even better chance by keeping the eggs inside their bodies till they have grown into tiny frogs. But it's finding somewhere to store the eggs while they grow that's the tricky part.

The Australian frog called *Rheobatrachus silus* swallows her own eggs and stores them in her stomach. The eggs grow into young froglets, which climb back up their mum's throat and hop out of her mouth.

In the Darwin frog, it's the father that looks after the eggs. He stores them for a while in a pouch in his mouth that he usually uses for singing. When the froglets have grown, he opens his mouth and out they hop. He also gets his croak back. The father midwife toad wraps strings

of eggs round his back legs. He looks after them until they are ready to hatch and then he takes them to a pond. He backs into the water, the eggs hatch and the tadpoles swim away.

Some mothers, like the pipa toad, stick their eggs on to their backs. The eggs sink into the skin. They then turn into tadpoles, which break out of the skin when they are ready.

GROWING UP

The change from egg to tadpole to a proper grown-up shape is called 'metamorphosis'. Morph means shape. But some amphibians never change from tadpole to grown-up. Like Peter Pan they stay young for ever. The axolotl looks like a large tadpole and should grow into a salamander.

But the water it lives in stops this happening and it stays a tadpole. Normal tadpoles can't lay eggs, but the axolotl can. The eggs grow into more axolotls, and there are never any grown-ups to boss the tadpoles about!

Sometimes tadpole life can be very short. The water-holding frog of Australia lives in the desert. When it rains the frogs lay their eggs in puddles. The tadpoles have to grow into frogs before the puddles dry out. The biggest tadpole often eats it brothers and sisters. As the last of the water dries up the young and old frogs fill themselves up till they look as if they could burst. Then they dig down into the soil and make a small room for themselves. They grow a special skin like a polythene bag to keep the water in, and they can stay like that for two years till it rains again. Thirsty Aborigines dig the frogs out and squeeze a drink from them. Do you fancy a glass of frog juice?

Factfile **Amphibian Words**

Frog-spawn
A collection of frog's eggs covered in jelly.

Lungs
The part of the body used for breathing.

Metamorphosis
The way in which an animal changes from an egg to an adult.

Ribs
The bones in an animal's chest that help protect its lungs.

Tadpole
The young frog that hatches from an egg.

Warty skin
A skin covered in lumps.

Can you match the name of the amphibian with its picture?

CAECILIAN WORM   **TOAD**   **NEWT**

SALAMANDER   **FROG**

Answers on page 92

Chapter 3

Snappers and Coilers
Reptiles

What is a reptile?
A reptile is an animal with a backbone. It breathes air and has a waterproof skin covered in scales.

REPTILE HISTORY

Millions of years ago reptiles ruled the world. Huge dinosaurs lived on land, enormous reptiles like giant bats flew in the sky and great lizard-like fish swam in the sea. But 65 million years ago almost all the reptiles died. No one knows quite why. Only five kinds have stayed alive. They are crocodiles and alligators; lizards; snakes; tortoises and turtles, and, all by themselves, the tuataras.

You've heard of all of them except the tuataras, right? Well, tuataras are very slow-moving lizards that live on small islands close to New Zealand. They live in burrows that they share with seabirds called petrels. They don't appear to be very friendly, as sometimes the tuataras eat the birds' eggs and sometimes the birds eat the baby tuataras.

Tortoises' scales are very large; each scale grows in rings and the number of rings can be a help in telling the age of a tortoise. Because the scales make the skin waterproof, reptiles are able to live on land as well as in water. A waterproof skin helps stop them from drying out. The other thing that reptiles can do that has allowed them to move on to land is to lay eggs that have shells. All reptiles start life in an egg.

Reptiles are said to be 'cold-blooded'. This doesn't mean that their blood is always cold. It means that they can't heat themselves in the way that humans can. Humans use the food they eat to warm themselves. Reptiles have to go to warm places to heat themselves. For example, lizards sunbathe on rocks in the morning to warm up after the cool of the night; snakes find sunny spots on grass to warm themselves. If there are no warm places then reptiles become cold and they slow down. This is why most of the world's reptiles live in warm climates. In winter many reptiles hibernate and so escape the problem of trying to keep warm.

MOVING ABOUT

As well as trying to keep the right temperature, reptiles also have to move about. They can run, swim, fly, walk on water and hang upside down from the ceiling! Not all of them, of course, but certain reptiles can.

The black mamba snake races along at 25 k.p.h. (a good running speed for a person).

Crocodiles and alligators swim using their tails. They close their nostrils, ears and throat with special muscles so the water can't get in when they are swimming. All crocodiles swallow stones. Without the extra weight they would not be able to swim under water.

Most snakes swim well. The yellow-bellied sea snake swims at 1m. per second, faster than a person can swim away.

Lizards and snakes can't fly, but some can glide long distances. The draco lizard glides up to 15m. between trees using flaps of skin on each side of its body as wings. The paradise snake can glide up to 35m. from one tree to another by hollowing the underneath of its body. It floats on a cushion of air trapped by its body a bit like a hovercraft.

The basilisk lizard beats even a flying snake. It can run on top of water. It has long toes on its back legs and dashes across water to escape other animals. If it falls in it swims under water.

Geckos are small lizards that can climb up glass and can even hang from the ceiling. They can do this because their feet have tiny hairs, made of scales, that cling on to bumps in the ceiling. Geckos usually live in trees, where they use their climbing skills to catch insects or to escape from their enemies.

ESCAPE

Reptiles are very good to eat, so to avoid being eaten they have found an enormous number of different ways of escaping from their enemies.

Tortoises, terrapins and turtles don't run away. Instead they pull themselves inside their shells. The stinkpot turtle has a second line of defence: it can make a terrible smell that stops birds eating it.

Many lizards can cut off their own tails. Garden worms can do this trick too. Special muscles tear off the tail without harming the animal. The tail goes on wriggling for some time and while its enemy watches the tail, the lizard runs away to grow another one. The new tail is smaller than the old one and hasn't any bones in it. Some lizards have very brightly coloured tails to keep their enemies' attention.

The armadillo lizard cannot lose its tail. Instead it holds on to its tail with its mouth and rolls itself into a ball. Spiky scales on its back turn it into a kind of lizard-hedgehog. The chuckwalla lizard of North America runs into a crack in the rocks and puffs itself up so that it cannot be pulled out.

Snakes use all sorts of tricks to defend themselves.

The milk snake, which is harmless, has the same colours of stripes on its skin as the poisonous coral-snake. Other animals are fooled and leave milk snakes alone.

The hog-nosed snake of America pretends to be a rattlesnake and warns enemies to keep away by rattling its tail, just like the real thing. Many snakes hiss a warning not to come any closer. Of course, it's even better if your enemy doesn't see you at all. Many snakes have patterns on their scales which make them very difficult to see.

Some, like the sand viper and the dwarf puff adder, bury themselves in sand so that only their eyes and noses show.

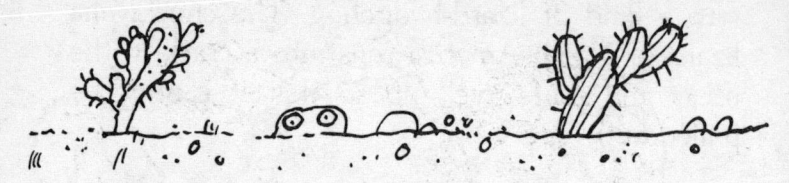

Even if they are found, snakes have more tricks. The grass snake pretends to be dead: it rolls on its back and sticks out its tongue just like a dead animal. Many animals will not eat dead meat as it could be bad, so they leave the grass snake alone.

SPLAT!

The rubber boa of Mexico hides its head under its body and waves its tail at its enemy. It prefers to have its tail bitten rather than its head.

POISON

If an enemy still attacks, then some snakes and two kinds of lizards can use a chemical for defence. This is poison or venom. Poison is a kind of spit or saliva. About a third of all snakes use poison either to defend themselves or to help them catch food.

The spitting cobra spits poison into the eyes of its enemy. It has a very good aim and can hit the eyes of an animal 2m. away. The poison is very painful and may make the attacker blind.

Most poisonous snakes use their teeth to bite the poison into their victims. The boomslang of Africa uses teeth at the back of its mouth to chew the poison in. It has to hold on while the poison trickles down grooves in the teeth.

Some snakes use hollow teeth, called fangs. Because these fangs are at the front of the mouth they are called front-fanged snakes. As these snakes bite, poison is pushed down through the teeth into the victim. This happens very quickly so the snake doesn't have to hold on for long. Once the poison is in, the snake can simply follow its victim at a safe distance and wait for the poison to work.

The king cobra is an example of a front-fanged snake. It grows up to 6m. long. Its poison can kill an elephant in four hours. When a king cobra is disturbed, it fans out a hood behind its head and it can raise its body till its head is taller than a person. People are very frightened of these large snakes, which kill 7,500 people in India each year.

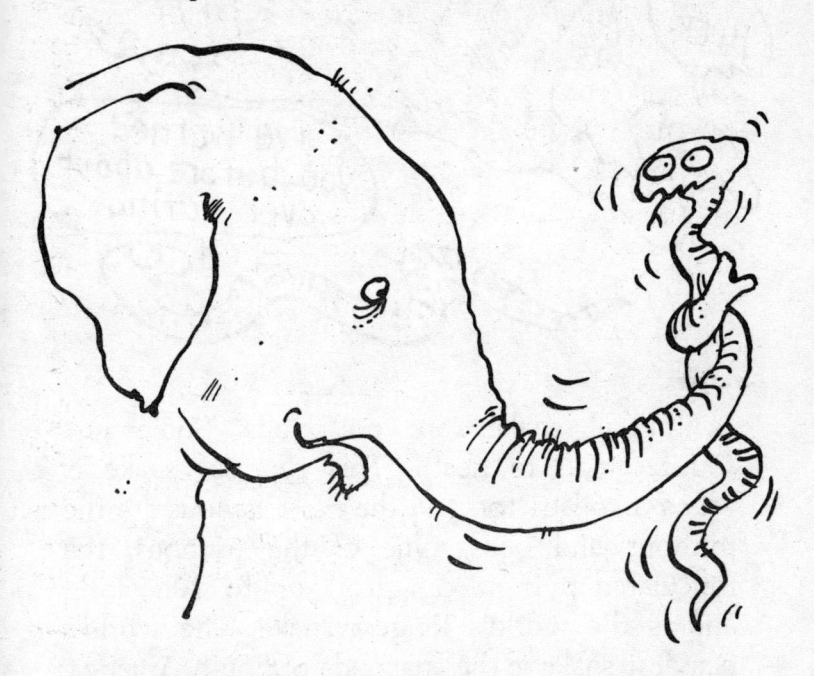

The country with the most poisonous snakes is Australia. It has the most poisonous land snake in the world, the inland taipan, and the most poisonous snake of all, the marine cobra, which lives in the sea close to the north-west coast of Australia. Perhaps that's why kangaroos jump all the time – to avoid the snakes!

Not all snakes are poisonous. Some just squeeze you to death. This type of snake is called a constrictor, and the most famous are the pythons and boas. One of the pythons, the reticulated python, can grow up to 10m. long and is the world's longest snake. The world's heaviest snake is the anaconda of South America. It lives in water and can grow to over 8m. long. A snake this large may measure over a metre round the thick part of its body.

FOOD

Constrictors don't crush their victims. Instead they wrap their bodies round the animal they have caught and squeeze till it can't breathe. Because snakes don't have any cutting teeth they have to swallow their food whole. Sometimes really large animals, like goats or deer, are swallowed by snakes. They can do this because their bottom jaws move apart. The jaw-bones are joined by an elastic part at the front; as the snake swallows, the jaws part and the snake forces its head over the animal it is swallowing. It's a bit like you being able to swallow a football! If a snake eats a really large animal it may be months before it eats again. One snake in a zoo went for over two years between meals.

The African egg-eating snake swallows eggs whole. The eggs are then pushed against special bones in its throat till they break. The snake then swallows the egg and spits out the shell. This may not sound very clever, but can you imagine swallowing an Easter egg without using your hands, and then spitting out the silver paper!

Even snakes, with their clever ways, have to catch food before they can swallow it. In fact, all the reptiles have to have ways of finding and catching food.

Lizards and snakes have good eyesight although snakes wear spectacles! Not glasses, but a special glass-like scale over their eyes to protect the eye from sand and dust; it's called a spectacle. Every few months the spectacles go milky and the snake becomes blind. This is because the snake's skin has worn out. It solves the problem by growing a new skin, but first it has to get rid of the old one.

The skin of a snake comes off in a single piece, like taking off a sock. As well as getting a fresh skin, the new spectacles are clear and the snake can see again. Lizards shed their skin in chunks. Crocodiles, tortoises and turtles lose small pieces of skin all the time, a sort of reptile dandruff.

The rattlesnake's rattle is made from pieces of old skin and gets bigger each time the snake sheds its skin. Up to a certain age you can tell how old a snake is by the number of rattles it has.

Snakes and lizards have a good sense of smell but they don't sniff smells like a dog. Instead they use their forked tongues to 'taste' smells in the air. The tongue is flicked in and out and then pressed into a special sensitive part of the snake's mouth.

Some snakes, like the rattlesnake and pit viper, can feel the heat from another animal. They have special places on their heads that measure the heat from small animals and, using heat as a guide, they can hunt mice and rats even in complete darkness.

Turtles have different ways of catching food. The matamata turtle lives in rivers. When it sees a fish, it opens its jaws so quickly that the fish is sucked in and swallowed. The alligator snapping turtle is even more cunning. Part of its tongue looks like a worm. It sits on the bottom of the river with its mouth open, wriggling the tongue to look like a worm. If a fish swims into its mouth to eat the worm, the turtle snaps shut its jaws and eats the fish instead.

Crocodiles can only snap their jaws shut, they can't chew. When they catch a big animal they hold on and pull the animal under water until it drowns. Then they snap their jaws on to a big piece of its body and roll over and over, tearing off a large piece of meat. They swallow the chunks that come off, whole.

EGGS

All reptiles hatch from eggs. Most hatch when the eggs are outside the mother. Sometimes the mother keeps the eggs inside her body. There, the young animals can grow safely, away from enemies. Just before the eggs are laid, the young animals break out of their eggs. They are born alive as miniature versions of their parents. This type of birth is called 'live birth'.

Sea snakes, which live in water all the time, give birth to live snakes, as eggs could not be laid in the water. Turtles, which also live in the sea, move on to the land to lay their leathery-shelled eggs in holes they dig on the beach. Most of the young are eaten by birds or other enemies as they try to run back down the beach and into the water.

Most reptiles bury their eggs and forget them, but there are some that look after their eggs.

Python mothers wrap their bodies around their eggs to protect them and keep them warm. Monitor lizards in Australia lay their eggs in termite mounds. The termites keep the eggs at the right temperature. After some time the monitor returns and digs out the young monitors that have hatched.

The temperature of the eggs is very important. Crocodile eggs that have been kept below 30°C grow into female animals, but eggs that have been kept above 33.9°C grow into male animals. Crocodile mothers look after their eggs. When the young hatch they call to the mother, who digs them out of the sand which covers them. She then carries the young in her huge jaws to the water.

The mother crocodile can hear her young and so can help them. Snakes aren't so lucky. Snakes are all deaf, so they can't hear their young or anything else. Snake-charmers who play music to snakes are not being listened to. The 'charm' that controls the snake is the movement of the pipe that is being played, not the music. Even when the poor snake is exhausted from dancing it can't close its eyes and go to sleep because it hasn't got eyelids. It has to sleep with its eyes open.

Factfile **Reptile Words**

Constrictor
The kind of snake that squeezes, instead of using poison, to kill other animals.

Dinosaur
Reptiles that used to live on Earth millions of years ago. Dinosaur means 'terrible lizard'.

Fang
A long sharp tooth, which may be hollow like a needle.

Front-fanged
Snakes which have fangs at the front of their mouths.

Hibernation
A special kind of sleep which lasts for a long time.

Saliva
A scientific name for spit.

Spectacle
The thin layer of skin over a snake's eyes.

Can you name each reptile and match each illustration with the correct description?

1

A REPTILE WITH A HARD SHELL

2

A REPTILE THAT POISONS THINGS

3

A REPTILE THAT CUTS OFF ITS OWN TAIL

4

A REPTILE THAT DROWNS THINGS

5

A REPTILE THAT SQUEEZES THINGS

Answers on page 92

Chapter 4

Feathers and Flight
Birds

What is a bird?
A bird is an animal which has a backbone and feathers. Humans have backbones too but, even if we had feathers, we couldn't fly because we are too heavy.

BIRD BODIES

Birds need to be light to fly so their bodies are different from ours.

They have hollow bones, which are very light. A frigate-bird's skeleton weighs less than its feathers. Birds can't have teeth, because teeth need heavy jaws to rest in, so instead they have beaks.

Beaks can be long and thin or short and fat — in fact, almost any shape. The important thing is that they are just the right shape for a certain way of feeding.

Birds that feed on creatures buried in mud have long thin bills to reach them. Birds that feed on meat have sharp curved beaks for tearing.

Birds use up a lot of energy and so their hearts have to beat much faster than ours. A human heart beats about 70 times a minute. A robin's heart beats about 570 times a minute, and a North American humming-bird's heart trips along at 1,000 beats a minute.

Pitter-patter-pitter-patter-pitter-patter-pitter-patter-pitter-patter-pitter-patter-pitter-patter-pitter-patter-pitter-patter-pitter...

EYES AND EARS

Birds need to find out about the world around them, so they have eyes and ears, but most birds do not use their sense of smell — except the king vulture, which feeds by smell.

Birds are supposed to have good eyesight, but it depends on the bird. Buzzards have eyesight eight times better than ours and can pick out a rabbit two miles away. Small birds have eyesight three times worse than ours, which may help explain why they sometimes collide with windows.

Different birds use their eyes in different ways. Birds that hunt, like owls, have eyes at the front of their head. Birds that are hunted, like the woodcock, have eyes on the sides of their head. They can see everything behind them without moving so it's very difficult for enemies to creep up on them.

Birds have different ways of hearing too. Lapwings can hear worms burrowing in the ground, and owls can hear mice moving in total darkness, but they can't hear the lowest note on a piano.

Owls don't often play the piano so it doesn't matter, but they do fly, and for that they need feathers.

FEATHERS

Feathers are only found on birds. There are three main types. Flight feathers are used for the wings and tail. Contour feathers cover the rest of the body. Down feathers are found under the contour feathers and are used to keep the bird warm.

Flight and contour feathers are the kind that you might find on the beach or in a park.

When birds preen (rub their bills through their feathers) they are hooking the feathers back into shape. Down feathers are very fluffy. This helps them trap a layer of warm air close to the bird, which keeps the bird warm. Eiderdowns, duvets or downies are filled with down feathers from ducks or geese. That's how the name came about, because originally it was down from eider ducks that was used. Don't worry — the down is collected from the nests, not the birds. Eiders use the down to keep their eggs warm as well as themselves.

Birds need a lot of feathers. A whistling swan has over 25,000, the ruby-throated hummingbird, which only weighs 3g., has just 940 feathers.

Birds take great care of their feathers. They can make their feathers waterproof by spreading oil on them. The oil is made in a special gland near the tail.

Cleaning is important, so some birds wash themselves by splashing in water, or they can use dust instead. Sparrows often dust themselves in small dips they make in dry soil. Herons use a powder made in special powder-puffs on their bodies to clean fish slime from their feathers. Some birds get help from others. Pigeons help each other look after their feathers. Other birds use different animals. Jays let ants crawl over their wings; the ants squirt acid on the feathers and this kills off insects living as parasites amongst the feathers.

Even with all this care, feathers wear out and have to be replaced by growing new ones.

Birds tend to replace their feathers in pairs, one on each side of the body at the same time. This means they don't become lopsided and fly round in circles.

NESTS

All birds have feathers and nearly all birds build nests. The biggest nest made of twigs is made by the bald eagle. It can be as high as 6m. and weigh nearly 2 tonnes. The birds can't manage all that building in one year and just add a bit to an old nest from last year. Some nests are over 100 years old.

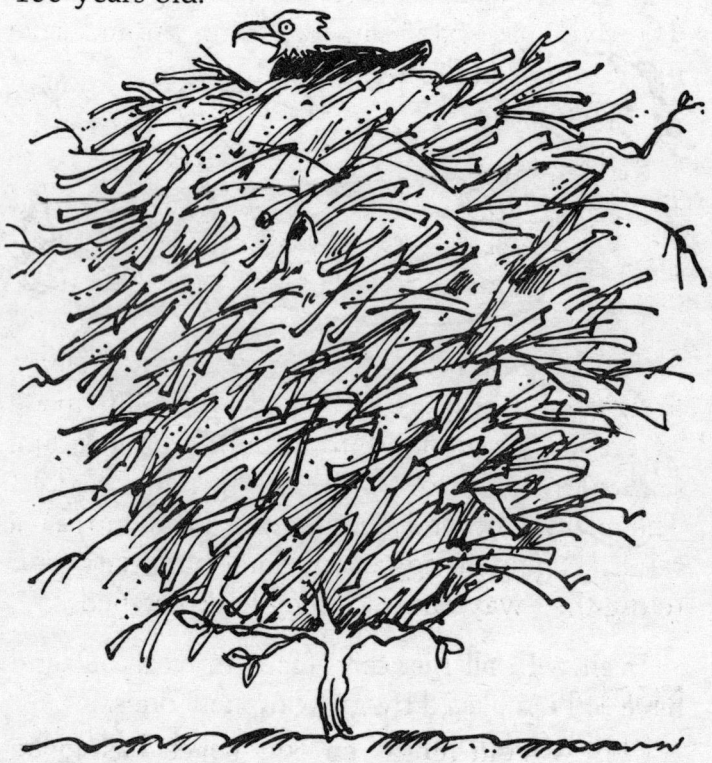

The smallest nest is made by the bee humming-bird. It is made of lichen, cotton and spiders' webs.

The white nest swiftlet makes a nest about the size of a hand using dried spit (saliva). If that sounds revolting, just wait. The nests are collected and boiled into soup by the Chinese. They have been eating bird's nest soup for over 1,000 years.

Some birds don't make a nest at all. The fairy tern lays its eggs in a fork of two branches of a tree, or even just balanced on a single branch. The chick has sharp claws to hang on and save itself from falling to the ground.

The biggest nest of any bird is not really a nest, more a heap of earth and plants. It's made by Freycinet's mound bird. It builds mounds 5m. high and 12m. across, with an egg in the middle. The plants rot and the mound heats up as a result, keeping the egg warm. Some birds die trying to dig their way out once they have hatched.

EGGS

All birds begin life as an egg which has to be kept warm. Most birds don't use mounds; instead they use the heat of their own bodies (incubation).

Usually both the mother and father bird look after the egg, but in emus it is the father that keeps the eggs warm. He looks after them for two months. He doesn't eat or drink for all that time and he loses a lot of weight.

Emperor penguins live on ice. As soon as the mother lays her single egg, the father moves it on top of his feet and covers it with his feathers. The mother then leaves to go fishing in the sea, which is miles away; she doesn't return until the egg has hatched. She feeds the chick on the fish she has caught and only *then* can the father go and fish for himself. Many fathers never reach the sea.

Cuckoos use other birds to look after, or foster, their eggs and to feed their chicks. They lay eggs that look like the foster-parents' eggs. The cuckoo eggs hatch first and the young cuckoo pushes all the other eggs out of the nest. The foster-parents then feed the cuckoo chick, which sometimes becomes much bigger than its foster-parents.

FOOD

Feeding is important to all animals, and birds have found many different ways to feed themselves.

A finch in the Galapagos Islands pecks the feathers of larger birds and drinks the blood that appears.

The green heron is a fishing bird. It puts an insect or a feather on the water of a pond and waits. Soon a fish comes to investigate and the heron snaps it up.

Frigate-birds don't just wait for fish; they catch flying fish whilst they are in the air.

White pelicans go in for team-fishing. They frighten fish by beating their wings and the fish are driven into the middle of a group of pelicans. They then dip their bills into the water and scoop up the fish.

Some scientists used to think that because humans used tools we were different from other animals. But since then many animals have been found that use tools, and some of them are birds.

The woodpecker finch has a short tongue and cannot reach insect grubs which have tunnelled into tree-trunks. Instead it uses grass-stems held in its beak to spear the grubs and pull them out.

Egyptian vultures pick up stones and use them to crack open ostrich eggs. The vultures are very poor shots and need a lot of attempts to crack open an egg.

A better way of breaking into a hard thing is to pick it up and drop it from a great height. Several birds use this way of doing things.

The lammergeyer vulture picks up bones and flies off with them. It drops the bones on to rocks, where they break open. The birds feed on the marrow of the bones and on small pieces of bone.

Herring-gulls do the same with shells. In seaside towns many of the shells you find on the pavement have not been washed in by the tide but have fallen from the sky! Another collection of shells you might find are piles of snails' shells in a wood. The shells are usually next to a stone, which a song-thrush has used to break open the snails before eating them. The stone is called the song-thrush's anvil.

Some birds have turned into thieves and get others to do the hard work for them. Black-headed gulls steal worms from lapwings. Frigate-birds attack boobies and make them disgorge the fish they have caught. The frigate-birds then eat the fish. Arctic skuas are mean to their fellow birds, not only eating their eggs but also forcing them to give up catches of fish they may be carrying.

Whatever way a bird chooses to feed, it will only stay alive if there is food to eat. If food disappears from one place, birds have to move to find food somewhere else.

TRAVEL

Birds have an amazing ability to travel huge distances to find food, mates or a place to nest.

The Arctic tern is the record holder for bird migration. Each year the bird flies 20,000km. from the Arctic, where it nests, to the Antarctic, and another 20,000km. back again. Because it is following the sun, it only sees the sun set for four months of the year.

Swifts are record holders too. They leave

their nests and don't touch the ground again until they build their own nests, when they are two or three years old. They even sleep while they are flying.

But it's not just how far they go that makes birds outstanding travellers.

Birds have an amazing sense of direction. Bristle-thighed curlews fly each year from Alaska to the tiny islands of Hawaii or Tahiti; that's about 9,000km., most of it over the sea, and without a map.

House-martins can fly from Scotland to Africa, then back again, and still manage to find the same nest they were born in.

As well as navigating using the sun, birds use the pattern of stars in the sky to tell them where to go. They can fly almost as high as a jumbo jet, as fast as a family car, as slowly as a person walking, and humming-birds can even fly backwards and upside-down.

Factfile **Bird Words**

Contour feather
A feather which helps give a streamlined shape to a bird's body.

Disgorge
A special way of being sick. Birds store food in a crop (pouch) and they can sick this food up to feed their young, or to give to robbers.

Down feather
A feather which keeps a layer of warm air close to a bird's body.

Flight feather
A feather used to give shape to a bird's wings and tail.

Incubation
The time when the eggs are kept warm by the bird so that the chick can develop in the egg.

Migration
The journey of a bird from one place to another at a certain time of year.

Preening
When birds use their bills to repair their feathers. They either nibble the feathers or pull them through their beaks.

Match the birds with the correct kind of beak and the kind of food they eat.

Answers on page 93

1 A beak that's good for tearing

2 A beak that's good for poking

BIRD

Blackbird

Eagle

Parrot

Heron

3 A beak that's good for stabbing

4 A beak that's good for cracking

FOOD

Meat

Fish

Worms, Insects

Nuts, Seeds

Chapter 5
Horns and Hair
Mammals

What is a mammal?
A mammal breathes air, has a backbone, feeds its young on milk and is the only animal with true hair. Most mammals give birth to live young. The only two that don't are the echidna, which looks like a hedgehog, and the duck-billed platypus; both of these mammals lay eggs. Mammals have larger brains than other animals and the mammal with the cleverest brain, or so we think, is the human.

Given a list of the things that mammals have in common, you might ask what does the average mammal look like? The answer is, there is no average mammal.

MAMMAL BODIES

Mammals can fly, like a bat, or swim, like a dolphin or a whale. They can be very large, like a hippopotamus, or very small, like a mouse. Or they can look exactly like us.

There are about 4,000 types of mammal and many of these are world-record holders. The largest, heaviest, tallest and smallest animals are all mammals, so finding an average shape is impossible.

MAMMAL SIZE

Let's look at size. The biggest mammal that lives on land is the African elephant. The biggest one ever shot weighed over 10 tonnes. The smallest mammal is Kitti's hog-nosed bat, which weighs less than 2g. It would take about 6,000,000 bats to equal the weight of that one elephant.

Even an elephant is small compared with the largest mammal of all, the blue whale. Blue whales can grow to be over 30m. long and weigh 190 tonnes, as much as nineteen elephants. You might think that such a huge animal would eat big fish, but in fact it eats tiny shrimp-like animals called krill. Blue whales have lost their teeth and have replaced them with strainers like fine combs which hang down from the roof of their mouths. They use the combs, called baleen, to separate the krill from seawater. Krill might be small, but a whale can eat the weight of a car in krill at one meal.

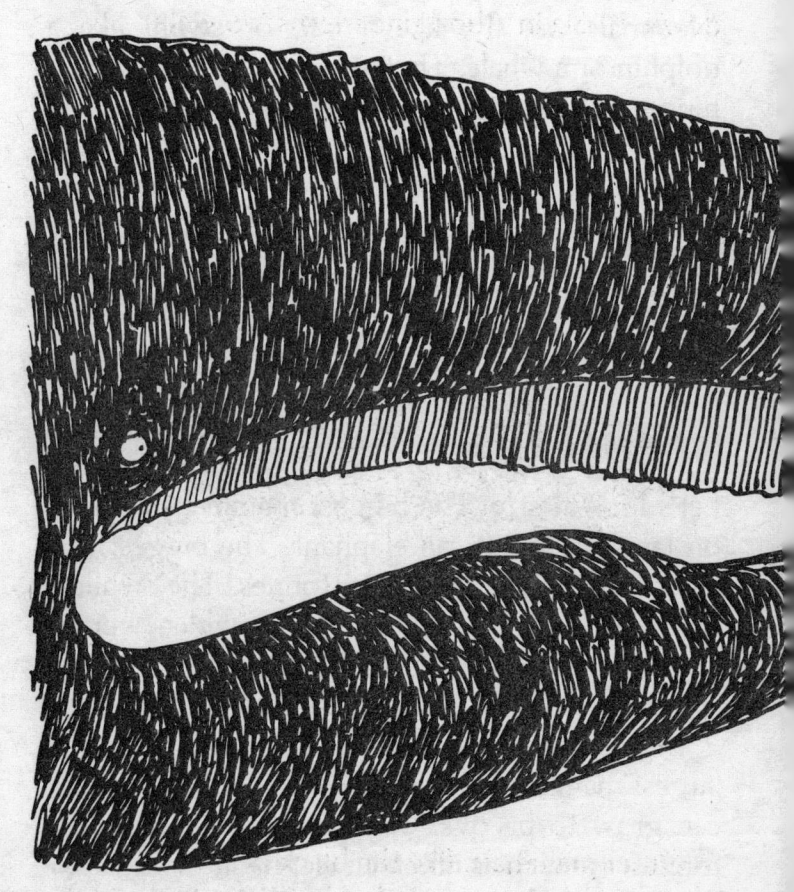

FEEDING

Mammals eat all kinds of food. Some, like koalas, have a boring time and eat only one kind of food. Koalas must like eucalyptus leaves, because that's all they eat. The leaves are quite juicy so they don't even have a drink to wash them down. Koala in Aborigine means 'no water'.

Other mammals, like the black bear of America, eat a whole range of food: fish, mice, young deer, fruits, nuts, berries and, of course, honey.

Ants are delicious if you happen to be an ant-eater. Several kinds of mammals eat ants. The giant ant-eater can stick out its tongue 60cm. into an ants' nest. Its tongue is covered in tiny spines and it's very sticky. Ants stick to the tongue and are pulled out of their tunnels. An ant-eater can pick up 500 ants in one lick.

A giraffe has a pretty long lick too, with its 45cm. tongue, as it munches its way through tree-leaves. Its head is in the trees because giraffes are the tallest animals on Earth. The tallest one ever shot was 5.8m. tall, taller than a double-decker bus. Giraffes have a difficult time drinking and have to spread their front legs wide to reach the water. Special valves in their necks stop blood rushing to their heads and making them faint. When they stand up they have the opposite problem, so they have a powerful heart to pump blood up to their heads.

Moles have no problems with height as they live underground. They dig long tunnels through the soil, then they run along the tunnels collecting worms that have fallen into them and can't get out again. The worms are stored in special larders. The mole bites the worm along its body; this doesn't kill the worm but stops it wriggling away. Moles can store hundreds of chewed worms in a larder, but they need them all because a mole eats its own weight in worms every day. Can you imagine eating your own weight in food every day? Difficult, even if it was chocolate biscuits and ice-cream.

Shrews, which are smaller than moles, need to eat every two to three hours or their stomachs start to dissolve and the inside of their bodies turn to jelly. As a rule, the smaller you are the more you have to eat compared with your own weight, and the more often you have to eat.

A blue whale may eat tonnes of krill at a time but it only eats for six months of the year. The rest of the time it diets, using up its fatty blubber.

Mammals eat almost everything there is to eat on Earth. But one has a very special food. It eats only blood! It is the much-feared vampire bat. Vampire bats do not suck blood from their victims like film vampires; instead they make a cut in the skin of their victim with their very sharp teeth and then they lap up the blood as it runs out. Vampire bats are small with mouse-sized bodies. They usually drink the blood of farm animals that are resting or are asleep, but sometimes a sleeping human has their blood taken.

Each bat drinks about five teaspoons of blood a day. You might think this is not enough to worry about. The reason for the fear is that as the bat drinks it may give its victim a disease called rabies, which will almost always kill it.

But don't panic! Vampire bats live in South America and besides, most bats eat insects. So there is no need to worry about bat bites.

MOVEMENT

Pumas or mountain lions live in North and South America. If you were being chased by one of these, you might try to escape by climbing a tree. Unfortunately this would not help, as pumas can jump 5.5m. up into the branches of a tree and then they are skilled climbers. They can also pounce 20m. to the ground without hurting themselves. If an African cheetah were chasing you, you might try running. Sadly you wouldn't stay ahead for long as the cheetah can run at about 100 k.p.h. A world-record sprinter only manages about 36 k.p.h. In fact the cheetah is not only the fastest mammal, it's also the fastest animal that lives on land.

The fastest mammal on two legs rather than four is the red kangaroo of Australia. Kangaroos can bound along at 56 k.p.h. for short distances. They are also very good at the long jump. One has leapt over 12m. in a single bound. Kangaroos belong to a special group of mammals called marsupials. Marsupials are mammals that bring up their young in pouches. Kangaroos give birth to tiny babies that crawl through their mother's fur and into the pouch on her tummy. Once inside, the baby holds on to a nipple with its mouth and drinks its mother's milk. A baby kangaroo, called a joey, stays in the pouch until it's about two months old. It still goes back into the pouch for milk and protection until it's about seven months old. Kangaroos aren't the only marsupials. There are marsupial mice, cats, rats and a bear, the koala.

The slowest mammal is the three-toed sloth. It's a bear-like creature that lives in trees. It hangs upside-down from the branches using huge claws on its arms and legs. Sloths move very slowly at about 2m. a minute. Because they spend all their lives upside-down, their fur hangs down from their tummies to their backs. Algae, which is a kind of plant, grows in their fur. This gives them a green colour, which helps hide them from their enemies.

COLOURS AND PATTERNS

If an animal is difficult to see we say it is camouflaged. Many mammals have colours or patterns that are used for camouflage. Polar bears are white, so they are difficult to see against snow and ice. Polar bears aren't worried about being seen by their enemies; the purpose of their camouflage is so that the seals they are trying to catch won't see them.

Tigers are striped for the same reason. Tigers hunt in forests, and when they are hiding in shadows or in long grass, their stripes make them difficult to see.

Some mammals can change their coat colour at different times of the year. The Arctic fox, stoat and mountain hare, for example, all have white fur in winter and brown fur in summer.

Some animals try to stand out from their surroundings. They want to be seen. The skunk has a bright black and white body which acts as a signal to stay away. If you don't, the skunk sprays a terrible-smelling liquid. It doesn't miss even if you are 3m. away.

Zebras have black and white coats like the skunk, but this time the bright stripes are not a warning but a special kind of defence. When an enemy like a lion attacks a herd of zebras, they run off together. Lots of stripy zebras running makes a confusing picture and the lion finds it difficult to pick out one particular zebra to attack. While the lion is thinking about it, the zebras escape.

DEFENCE

Instead of running away, some mammals stay still. In fact, the opossum stays very still. It pretends to be dead. 'Playing possum' is a phrase that means playing dead.

Some animals roll into a ball. The armadillo has armour-plates made of bone and leathery skin. Once it has rolled itself up, few enemies can get through its defence.

The hedgehog uses spines to protect itself, but the most impressive mammal with spines is the porcupine. It is covered in long hollow hairs called quills. When it is attacked it can run backwards into an enemy. The tips of the quills stick in the enemy and break off. The tips then work their way into the body of the attacker and may cause death a long time later.

Some mammals don't live alone like the porcupine, but in groups. Elephant herds are strictly for ladies only. Each herd consists of mothers and their children, plus old and young ladies. If they are attacked the young elephants hide behind their mums, who all get close to each other.

In baboons it's the fathers who fight attackers whilst the mothers carry the children to safety.

Dolphins will help defend each other by attacking sharks with their pointed beaks. Dolphins have been known to lift injured divers to the surface. This is not so odd when you know that dolphins lift other injured dolphins to the surface so they can breathe.

Now a question for you: Which mammal, living on Earth, can run at 36 k.p.h., can jump the height of a door, can swim, and has flown at 39,897 k.p.h. in space and invented television and baked beans? **Answer on page 93**

Factfile **Mammal Words**

Algae
A very simple kind of plant. The slime in ponds and fish-tanks is made of algae.

Baleen
A sieve made of whalebone that hangs down from the roof of a whale's mouth.

Camouflage
The markings or colour which make an animal look like its surroundings.

Eucalyptus
A kind of tree that grows in Australia.

Krill
A shoal of shrimp-like creatures.

Marsupial
An animal which has a pouch in which it raises its young.

Quill
The hollow hair of a porcupine.

Rabies
A disease which kills animals, including humans. It is caused by a virus.

Some animals have been walking in the snow. Can you match the animal with its proper track? Which one is not a mammal?

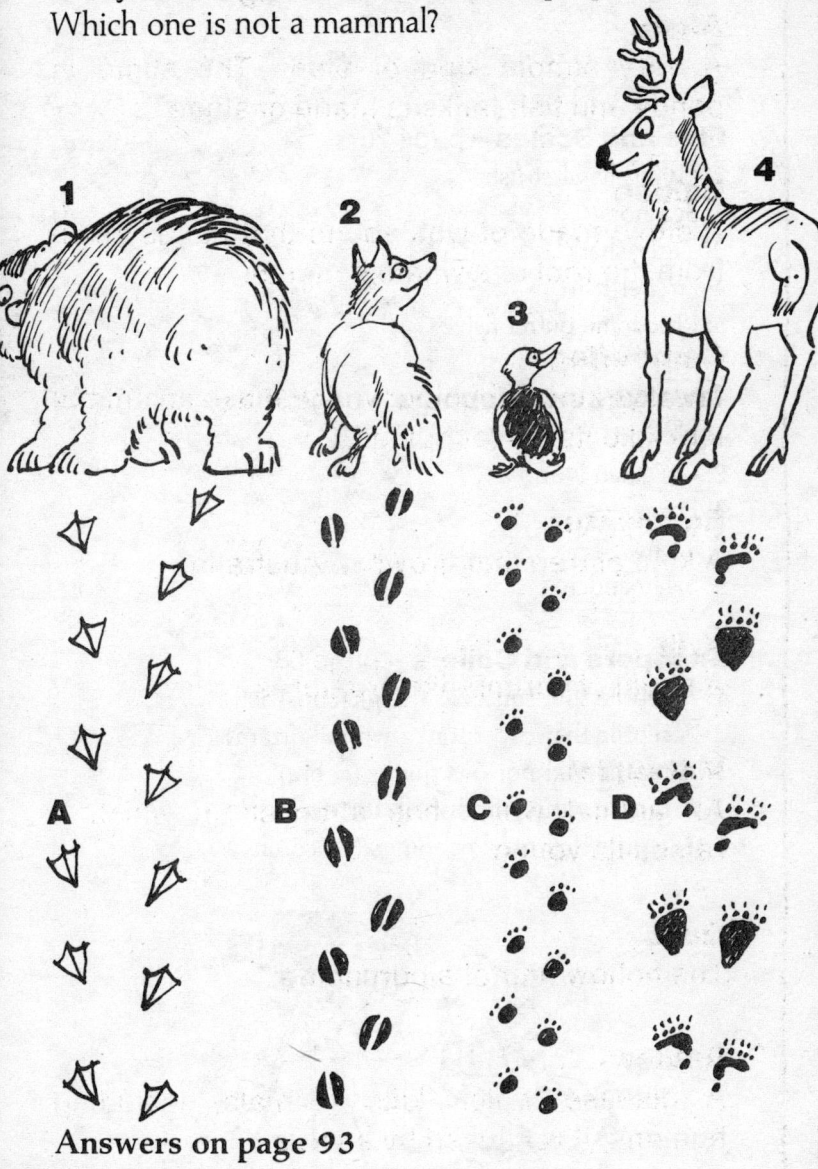

Answers on page 93

Answers

Fins and Scales – page 26
1: Flying hatchet fish
2: Sea-horse
3: Tiger-shark
4: Archer-fish
5: Porcupine puffer fish

Croakers and Hoppers – page 38
1: Newt
2: Caecilian worm
3: Frog
4: Toad
5: Salamander

Snappers and Coilers – page 58
1: A reptile that squeezes things (constrictor)
2: A reptile that cuts off its own tail (lizard)
3: A reptile that poisons things (cobra)
4: A reptile with a hard shell (tortoise)
5: A reptile that drowns things (crocodile)

Feathers and Flight – pages 74–5
1: Bird: eagle; food: meat
2: Bird: blackbird; food: worms, insects
3: Bird: heron; food: fish
4: Bird: parrot; food: nuts, seeds

Horns and Hair – page 89
The mammal that lives on Earth, can run at 36 k.p.h., can jump the height of a door, can swim, and has flown at 39,897 k.p.h. in space and invented television and baked beans is a **HUMAN**!

Horns and Hair – page 91
1: (bear) Track D
2: (fox) Track C
3: (duck) Track A
4: (deer) Track B

The **duck** is not a mammal.

Index

African elephant, 77, 88
alligator, 40, 42
alligator snapping turtle, 53
anaconda, 50
ant, 80
ant-eater, 80
arawana, 20
archer-fish, 20
Arctic fox, 86
Arctic skua, 71
Arctic tern, 71
armadillo, 88
armadillo lizard, 45
arrow frog, 31
Atlantic torpedo ray, 16
axolotl, 35, 36

baboon, 89
bald eagle, 66, 74
basilisk lizard, 43
bat, 77
beak, 60
bee humming-bird, 66
bird's nest soup, 67
black bear, 79
black-headed gull, 71
black mamba snake, 42
blackbird, 74
blood, 82
blue whale, 77, 82
boa, 47, 50
bony fish, 8, 10, 11, 12

boobies, 71
boomslang, 48
Brazilian blacksmith frog, 33
bristle-thighed curlew, 72
buzzard, 62

caecilian, 28
cartilage, 8, 24
cheetah, 83
chuckwalla lizard, 45
cichlid fish, 22
cold-blooded, 41
colour, 14, 31–33, 44, 45, 85–87
constrictor, 50, 57
contour feather, 63, 64, 65
coral-snake, 45
crocodile, 40, 42, 52, 54, 56
cuckoo, 68

Darwin frog, 35
dinosaur, 39, 57
discus fish, 21
dolphin, 77, 89
dolphin fish, 13
down feather, 63, 64, 65
draco lizard, 43
duck-billed platypus, 76
dwarf puff adder, 46
dwarf pygmy goby, 9

echidna, 76

egg-eating snake, 51
Egyptian vulture, 70
eider duck, 64
electric eel, 17
electric ray, 16
emperor penguin, 68
emu, 68

fairy tern, 67
fang, 48, 49, 57
fin, 12
flight feather, 63, 64, 65
flying fish, 12
flying hatchet fish, 12
flying lizard, 43
flying snake, 43
Freycinet's mound bird, 67
frigate-bird, 59, 69, 71
frog, 27–37
front-fanged snake, 48, 49, 57

gecko, 43
giant ant-eater, 80
gill, 24, 29
giraffe, 80
grass snake, 32, 46
great white shark, 19
green heron, 69, 74

heartbeat, 61
hedgehog, 88
heron, 65, 74
herring-gull, 70
hibernation, 42, 57
hippopotamus, 77
hog-nosed snake, 45
hollow bones, 59
horrida, 14
horse, 82
house-martin, 72
humming-bird, 61, 72

incubation, 67, 73
inland taipan, 49

jawless fish, 8, 24
jay, 65
joey, 84

king cobra, 49
king vulture, 61
Kitti's hog-nosed bat, 77
koala, 79, 84
krill, 78, 90

lammergeyer vulture, 70
lamprey, 8
lapwing, 62
lion, 87
lizard, 40, 41, 43, 45, 47, 52, 53
lung-fish, 20

marine cobra, 49
marsupial, 84, 90
matamata turtle, 53
metamorphosis, 35, 37
midwife toad, 35
migration, 71–73
milk snake, 45
mole, 81
monitor lizard, 55
mountain hare, 86
mouse, 77
mouth-breeder, 22
mud skipper, 20

newt, 27, 30, 32

opossum, 87
ostrich, 70
owl, 62

paradise snake, 43

parrot, 74
pelican, 69
penguin, 68
petrel, 40
pigeon, 65
pipa toad, 35
piranha, 19
pit viper, 53
poison, 13–15, 31–33, 47–50
polar bear, 85
porcupine, 88
preen, 63, 73
puffer fish, 13, 24
puma, 83
python, 50, 55

quill, 88, 90

rabies, 83
rattlesnake, 45, 52, 53
red kangaroo, 83
reticulated python, 50
Rheobatrachus silus, 34
robin, 61
rubber boa, 47
ruby-throated humming-bird, 64

salamander, 27, 30, 31
sand viper, 46
scale, 9, 10, 25, 40, 45
scorpion-fish, 14
sea snake, 55
sea-horse, 23
seal, 85
shark, 10, 11, 18, 19
shrew, 81
skin, 10, 27, 28, 29, 39, 52

skunk, 86
snake, 40–43, 45–53, 55–57
song-thrush, 71
sparrow, 64
spectacle, 52, 57
spiny newt, 32
spitting cobra, 47
sting-ray, 15
stinkpot turtle, 44
stoat, 86
stone-fish, 14
swift, 71–72
swim-bladder, 10, 11, 25

teeth, 8, 10, 18–20, 48, 57, 60, 78
terrapin, 44
three-toed sloth, 84–85
tiger, 86
tiger-shark, 18
toad, 28, 30, 32, 33, 35
tortoise, 40, 44, 52
tuatara, 40
turtle, 40, 44, 52, 53, 55

vampire bat, 82

water-holding frog, 36
whale, 77
whale-shark, 9
whistling swan, 64
white nest swiftlet, 67
woodcock, 62
Woodhouse's toad, 33
woodpecker finch, 69

yellow-bellied sea snake, 43

zebra, 86, 87